People Magnet

How to Talk Effectively Quiet Your Mind and Become a People Magnet

(Build Powerful Relationships and Positively Impact the Lives of Everyone)

Leslie Martinez

Published By **Chris David**

Leslie Martinez

All Rights Reserved

People Magnet: How to Talk Effectively Quiet Your Mind and Become a People Magnet (Build Powerful Relationships and Positively Impact the Lives of Everyone)

ISBN 978-0-9948647-7-2

No part of this guidebook shall be reproduced in any form without permission in writing from the publisher except in the case of brief quotations embodied in critical articles or reviews.

Legal & Disclaimer

The information contained in this book is not designed to replace or take the place of any form of medicine or professional medical advice. The information in this book has been provided for educational & entertainment purposes only.

The information contained in this book has been compiled from sources deemed reliable, and it is accurate to the best of the Author's knowledge; however, the Author cannot guarantee its accuracy and validity and cannot be held liable for any errors or omissions. Changes are periodically made to this book. You must consult your doctor or get professional medical advice before using any of the suggested remedies, techniques, or information in this book.

Upon using the information contained in this book, you agree to hold harmless the Author from and against any damages, costs, and expenses, including any legal fees potentially resulting from the application of any of the information provided by this guide. This disclaimer applies to any damages or injury caused by the use and application, whether directly or indirectly, of any advice or information presented, whether for breach of contract, tort, negligence, personal injury, criminal intent, or under any other cause of action.

You agree to accept all risks of using the information presented inside this book. You need to consult a professional medical practitioner in order to ensure you are both able and healthy enough to participate in this program.

Table Of Contents

Chapter 1: The Secrets Of Self-Confidence And Charisma 1

Chapter 2: Tips For Making A Powerful First Impression 7

Chapter 3: What Can You Do To Start A New Conversation With Anyone 17

Chapter 4: How To Connect With People At A Moment's Notice 27

Chapter 5: Getting Ready To Speak In Public 38

Chapter 6: Destroy Your Social Fears And Learn Social Grace 42

Chapter 7: The Three Golden Rules Of Making New Friends 49

Chapter 8: Angry Spouse 55

Chapter 9: Anger Issues 63

Chapter 10: Anger And Men 70

Chapter 11: Anger And Forgiveness 77

Chapter 12: Male Anger Management ... 89

Chapter 13: Life, Character, Principles ... 96

Chapter 14: Achieving Manhood 105

Chapter 15: Maintaining Manhood 113

Chapter 16: What Is Value 121

Chapter 17: How To Become Valuable . 125

Chapter 18: What Is Money? 160

Chapter 19: Where Does Money Hide? 162

Chapter 20: What Can Buy Money? 168

Chapter 21: How Value Brings Money? 178

Chapter 1: The Secrets Of Self-Confidence And Charisma

Confidence and personality are the primary factors in your ability to talk and get along with others comfortably. It is impossible to feel comfortable in a conversation if are unsure of yourself or are unsure of your capacity to connect with others. Did you recall my tale from last time? Insecurity robs you your natural humor and capacity to come up with spontaneously original ideas when you respond.

If you're lacking confidence, you are more likely to think too much about what is being targeted towards you.

It is harder to respond to criticisms because you spend an instant in determining whether your low self-esteem has been shattered or impacted by the tone of the discussion. This means that people with low self-confidence will be more difficult than you would normally be to utilize all the most effective methods that you've acquired. It will be difficult to maintain how you speak which can lead to unintentional and inconvenient pauses that could cause you to lose control over the conversation.

An absence of confidence can make it impossible for you to be capable of exercising the influence you would otherwise exercise over the course of your conversations. If you're not sure of your abilities, the odds are that you'll being speaking from a state that is weak rather than strong. It can be more apparent in conversations and negotiations in which you could be pushed by colleagues who are quicker in absorbing their thoughts, and not weighed down by an absence of concentration.

Low confidence is not a criminal offense or life sentence, but it is. The fact that you are low on confidence doesn't affect your character over the long term. That doesn't mean you'll never have the ability to meet new people or convince people to love your personality. No! It's still possible to make an occasional acquaintance and occasional acquaintance, but you're losing ten opportunities to meet more people and make new acquaintances.

How do you determine when you're experiencing issues that are bordering on confidence?

There's no easy or exact method to determine whether someone is highly competent or not with regards to making connections and forming acquaintances. Most likely, however, you'll feel extremely shy. actually, you might have a difficult time walking towards strangers in order to engage in conversation even. A person who isn't confident will rarely will go the extra mile to engage in conversation with someone you're not familiar with. It is possible to give yourself many reasons to not engage in conversation with that person, however in the back of your head is the fact that the sole reason you're not doing it is because you're uncertain of your capacity to make the conversation lively and lively.

Are you finding it difficult to engage in conversation? Do you find your stomach at a halt every time you're talking to people you'd like to get to know? Do you have the confidence to meet the person you admire, begin off well, but then stop in mid-way through the opening? Are you forced excuses for yourself due to the fact that you thought you were bored or lost control over the conversations?

These are merely instances of scenarios typical to what people with low confidence in themselves and their charisma could be in lots of instances.

How do you address the issues of charisma and confidence?

Low confidence is only due to the fact that you've been influenced by that you are not who you appear to be. The lack of charisma comes as a result of untrue assertions are now persistent thoughts that are flying around throughout your mind. Similar to negative affirmations, when you let negative thoughts about yourself to run over a long period of time in your brain, they will eventually become concrete and you start to conform to their limitations on the person you are. If you keep underestimating the value of yourself and value yourself less, you'll be unable to alter your mindsets.

This is the only method to get rid of your lack of confidence and charisma and to change your thinking about your own self. Avoid entering an encounter doubting whether you are even there. If you require a good look or a new outfit, alter your clothes or perhaps something else.

Be sure to be the most comfortable you can be in your own skin. It is not good for anyone to constantly question yourself. Instead, feel comfortable with yourself.

Find yourself and accept yourself as you truly are. This will lead to getting a boost in your confidence. The tips you will find that follow are designed towards helping solve problems of confidence. Let's dive to them in the following chapter.

Chapter 2: Tips For Making A Powerful First Impression

First impressions, they affirm, is the longest lasting. In the case of making new connections and forming new relationships it is difficult to take into account the significance to ensure that your initial impression is one of a positive nature. You must go all out to make an impact in the first time you start a conversation with a brand stranger. I advise those I meet that they will have minimum of 10 seconds to impress their counterpart enough to make them be enticed to keep the conversation going. For the first few seconds, both sides look at each other, determined to come up with conclusions that determine the answers they give.

Impress everyone with your first impression. Get your partner or friends engaged, and you're almost halfway through forming an unforgettable conversation.

In contrast in the event that the initial impression they get about your character is not positive or they are able to sense that you might be snobby, cocky and rude, or unsure, or dull, they will begin to plan their next steps to make it clear that is just beginning. What can you do to make your first impression memorable? These are some ideas to assist you.

* Arrive punctual

A lot of people take their the time they have for granted and go according to their own schedules This is a good thing however only if you don't have specific time frames that you must adhere to when you meet with the needs of someone else. Don't ever be guilty for being apathetic with timing. Never show up one hour behind on a date. This sends a negative signal to your partner. This also means that you may must begin by making an apology that is blatantly professing. This is definitely not the best way to begin your day. would like to have when making new acquaintances. Don't leave someone hanging unless there are very compelling justifications for it. If that happens, ensure you text ahead and tell them reasons for being somewhat tardy. The best thing to do is just show up at the time you are.

Dress to suit don't dress in a way that is unsuitable. overdress.

It's not a secret that the way you're viewed is based on through the clothes you wear. Another little-known fact is that you could also alter the way others view your appearance by the way you look. This is not talking about fancy dress or telling you to pile over your Gucci or Prada collection. I'm simply asking you to dress well and present yourself in a professional manner. A meticulous attention to detail could bring you double the respect as what you'd normally get. A well-groomed appearance may not earn you a new acquaintance or find you a new friend However, at most, it's likely offer you the chance. If you don't dress well and you're already removed from the conversation by the time you've even put your head to the side of the table. The perfect appearance is not an option, it's essential.

One of the best things about being clean and well-groomed is that it's not as difficult as people believe it to be. The basics such as taking care to keep your nails and hair neatly trimmed maintaining your teeth and breath clean as well as wearing pressed gowns can do wonders for the appearance of your face and also your chances of creating a lasting impression.

In addition Make sure you have the proper notice to whatever function you're going to. It is not a good idea to look sloppy or overdressed to any gathering. Make sure you dress appropriately.

If you're unsure of what is regarded as being overdressed or undressed in a certain occasion, you should consider dressing up. It is possible to dress for a special occasion better than looking casual to a formal occasion.

For final considerations make sure you dress the most elegant way you are able without attempting at causing too much an uproar by dressing too extravagantly as much as you are able to. Always be neat and tidy. This gives you a clean playing field.

- Be exciting

It's true that no one likes dull conversations. If I approach you at a bar to let my problems out to you, I will likely find a way to leave as quickly as your legs will allow the weight of your body. If I'm dining at the table and I ramble on about work, you'll be able to switch off fairly quickly and your chances of having a an enjoyable conversation are gone prior to even beginning. Beware of the most serious offense of trying to engage in conversation "Boring, dead talk."

There is no need to worry if you have the best advice and referrals from a friend of a common acquaintance or business acquaintance If you talk for a short time and your partner's brain senses decide that this will turn out to be a very lengthy or very short conversation, you've missed the opportunity to make a memorable conversations. Everybody is like that. Everyone hates boring people when they are having a the table.

There is no way to teach anyone how to make you more interesting. You could think of a thousand humorous, short openers as well as 100 topics to consider on your next meet-up or date however, it will make a dull person. Every conversation, and the participants in it, are unique from all other conversations within the room, or in all of the world.

However, even if you've mapped out the scenario and practiced it many times over in your mind it is inevitable that conversations be different in the direction you had thought of.

It is important to be creative and witty all the time.

What is the solution to being boring? The answer is simple, dull people are either busy or boring. The solution is to get into the people you're talking with. If you're doing this in the right place, you'll notice when things are about to be boring and will take the necessary changes. Don't get so engrossed in your own thoughts that you can't be aware of when you are headed to a stop. Another thing to accomplish is broaden your perspectives. Learn daily new knowledge. Increase your knowledge of your life, and take an interest in different areas. There is no way to know that you'll be sitting alongside a pathologist who is chemical or florist. If your expertise is extensive it is possible to keep people captivated right from the beginning. This is logical, in fact.

* Keep eye contact

Within the first couple of minutes after meeting the person you've never met, they're looking at you and trying to determine how much of your attention they think you merit. A major turnoff which I've already said, is the lack of charisma and confidence. When you are lacking these characteristics immediately, you lose signals that everyone else has to interpret. One among the most evident signs by men is being competent at keeping eye contact.

If you are walking up to anyone, make sure you make sure to look them straight in the eyes. This gesture shows them that they are confident and you are aware of what you wish to achieve and you're not frightened by their presence.

Don't look back or down at the floor as you speak to your friends. Avoid staring blankly in their eyes, even though you are in a conversation. If you break the contact, it will take some time, but don't let it be obvious that you're avoiding eye contact. This is especially effective if you are a person who is shy, or perhaps is skeptical about your intentions. No matter what it's a proposal for business or job interview or even a romantic dinner. make sure that your eyes are doing all the lifting for you. Take a look at the person in front of you.

* Make sure you are clear and concise.

Each request that you submit is either granted or denied at some point; therefore why ramble on about your chest? It is appreciated to be clear in your goals. This increases your standing and informs those who you meet that you're someone who is aware of what they want.

Clear and concise communication helps people to relate to your thoughts and connect with your ideas.

You could gain new friends, admirers as well as supporters for whatever causes you're advocating for.

Chapter 3: What Can You Do To Start A New Conversation With Anyone

Then, you enter your favourite bar, and then you see someone who you'd like to chat with. The goal is set! However, there is a small issue. It's not like you've been acquainted with them or you're a complete stranger. Perhaps you're attending a technology event and a tech expert whom you've always been impressed by her online appearance walks by. What can you do?

Studies have shown that the majority of people back off or decide not to risk embarrassing situations and awkwardness in trying to communicate even. Some take the chance and then make an effort to ruin the entire incident in such a manner that they're not able to attempt it the next opportunity.

Very few people are skilled at engaging in new conversations with strangers.

Here are some tips to aid you to become an expert in launching new conversations.

* Design great One-line openers

If you're trying to conquer your shyness this is an excellent advice. Establish a routine you are able to trust. Make a couple of minutes every day to improve the one-line openers you use.

Punchlines are always a good idea When you choose the one that you've used numerous times, you get advantages of having a familiar face with your partner.

As an example, when I was a kid I used to have an open-ended bottle. Every time I entered the bar and saw people I'd like to chat with I went towards them and inquired "if I bought you the next glass, would you drink it as slowly as possible with me?"

In retrospect, the method sounds somewhat sloppy at the moment however, my method produced better than average results. As I was used to this, I could easily overlook the a instances when it did not work due to the sexiness or dullness of the topic. It is important to develop excellent one-liners specifically for social and intimate celebrations.

* Ask a question

Questions can be a fantastic method of capturing people's attention. Check out Amazon KDP to see if you'll find that sales material for bestsellers has action questions which draw readers? It is possible to work similar fashion with people. If you ask someone a question, they is required to respond giving you possibility of keeping the conversation going.

Even the most inconsiderate of people are likely to respond to questions that are a surprise, particularly in situations that demand their attention for just some time.

In this case, for example, you could say, "If you had to choose between free air tickets for the rest of your life and a million dollars, which would you go for?". The question requires your audience to consider their thoughts before presenting a answer. This response gives you the chance to make the connection stronger. The answer will usually be then followed by an introduction as well as some small talk. Utilize this advantage to your advantage in particular in situations where you aren't able to find an appropriate one-liner that can start your conversation.

Don't ask questions that are uneasy or personal questions.

This is a crucial point to stand by itself. Every kind of question is acceptable to begin a conversation but not those that are personal, or that make someone uncomfortable. It is not a good idea to allow walls that start to form on the minds of persons you're trying get to speak with. This is certainly not a good idea. Instead, make sure to ask open-ended questions which aren't interpreted as personal or offending.

Don't ask individuals about their weight, in particular or if you're creative enough to to transform that information into an amusing story.

If you're determined to be safe however, don't make a fuss about your personal details.

* Request the help you need, or even offer to assist

There are a myriad of methods for people to engage in conversation however this is the most secure ways to stay clear of an unintentional clap-back.

Asking for help is almost always met with favorable results.

When I was in Europe some time ago I had an exchange with a scientist. I asked, "If the Amsterdam airport had a shuttle service?" He did not know about it, but that's not the issue. I was trying to get him out from his shell and the question led him to talking with me. The conversation opened the way for us to talk about other subjects. Be extra secure by asking questions that someone else is likely to be interested in. There is the option of borrowing sheets of paper, pens and pens for jotting notes, or inquire about the postcode of your area to start the conversation. Then, you'll have the chance to begin the discussion.

A different approach is to be friendly to others around. Giving help to those who appear unclear or confused is sure to earn you a slack "thanks" at the very at. A good starting point for conversation if you're a master of you have your onions.

* Request an opinion

This is a direct analogy to the previous tip. Like you ask questions, opinions will get people you'd like to talk with, to talk to you in a minimal amount of effort. Perhaps it's harder to obtain opinions from people who are not even acquaintances. Why not leave the public's opinions, not personal ones.

Test this out for yourself. If you are at a local soccer game You might be able to ask "Many individuals believe Ronaldo is better over Lionel Messi, but Messi is as dedicated. If he weren't the case, he'd be at the top of football world without Ronaldo because of his physique."

If the person who is in the front of you is an avid football player There isn't a limit of the topics you could be discussing.

You have created the opportunity for you to be able to disagree with your opinion by not showing your personal opinion. Your opinion could be used increase the chances for you to talk with the other.

If you want to start conversations with a positive manner there are a few tips to help you maintain the flow of conversation.

* The five-second rule

If you're timid, this advice is perfect for you.

The five second rule since it is a requirement to take a the decision to speak or not with someone whom you recently met in just five minutes.

This way, you'll have the ability to take a decision quick, which cuts away the chance to put off decisions. You should decide within 5 seconds if you're going to start an exchange or not. If you choose to start a conversation begin a conversation, then take a stand immediately and then walk towards the person.

* Find common grounds quickly

Helpful suggestions, questions such as one-liners or questions are great ways to begin a conversation but they also can go out quickly when you fail to initiate the conversation right from the beginning. In order to avoid this, try for common ground whenever you can. This could mean a common acquaintance, having similar interests or even an opinion shared by both of you; however you are looking for, identify an interest or common ground to explore over a period of time until you discover something intriguing enough to talk about with the person you wish to talk with. It is the goal of conversations, after all. to talk about interesting topics and in a fun way.

* Do not close things.

Don't make statements that are too long and ask questions which put you in a bind. Do not respond to questions with pointing to the answer. Avoid answering "yes" or "No" for questions that need some more. One of the characteristics of an effective conversationalist is the capability to connect one topic with another, without losing the control over the whole discussion. Always be proactive to extend the conversation and continue the conversation.

Chapter 4: How To Connect With People At A Moment's Notice

Imagine that you've made it through the first stage. What can you do to get them excited about you to the point who want to see a similar show? How do you convince people to get to know your personality on a deeper degree? In the end, creating new friendships is based on the ability of you to show people you're worthy of having as friends. We will examine a few ways to increase the amount of people who are interested in your.

* Names! Names!! Names!! !

Are you hoping that people attempt to forget about you or not be interested in your work? Remind them of your name frequently. This will provide them with the desire to work hard not to be linked with your name. We take great satisfaction from our names. That's why we take the time to come up with new names to themselves. This is due to the desire to get that nickname frequently. When someone calls you by the name of someone it's almost an infraction to not remember that name, or to fall into the trap of calling them another name. It is essential to remember at minimum the initial name of those who you hope to engage in constructive conversation with. It will allow you to escape shades of discord from the beginning.

When you call people by their name during a conversation implies that you wish for conversations to be more intimate, one-onone or between acquaintances.

Be cautious in formal settings as you might require attaching the names with titles in order in order to make things more formal and organized. However, at all times, be aware that a man has pleasure in his name much more than other things. If you call him by the incorrect name and he is resentful. Repetition the error the next time, he will mentally write that you are not interested. concern for the matter. Another way to get rid of the reluctance that is associated with names is to make use of names frequently, right after they are explained to you. This will help you become familiar with the name as well as identifying the person standing in front of your with the name. There is a chance that you forget the name during a later meeting however, forgetting someone's name in the exact spot that it's given to you is unwise. In this regard, be alert when you're being exposed to people you have never met before.

* Be present

There you are engaged in conversation or in another obscurity. The people around you notice if you're at their side. There is nothing exciting for anyone to be disengaged or are not in present moment. This is an unending turnoff for those who are not able to remain focused on the present. If you desire to engage in excellent conversations, you shouldn't be just a few miles away from someone standing in front of you. It is possible to lose track of conversation, leading to embarrassing questions to clarify your thoughts or embarrassing interruptions that are easy to avoid.

Be careful not to get caught up in any incident that goes beyond the context of your discussion. Don't lose focus or get caught up throughout an exchange.

This is inconsiderate and rude to repeatedly repeat this.

Make sure you use the correct body language indicators

The words that are spoken from your mouth are just a fraction of the verbal language. Another portion is focused on your body language as you talk. Your body language could attract people or make people to leave. The body language can be a potent instrument (perhaps much more efficient than speaking) that will help to get people interested in your personality.

Your body language may indicate something completely different from the words you're using and yet people are able to determine what your body's trying to communicate as we're trained to interpret your body language as authentic gestures.

There is no way to be convincing anyone if your body language indicates that you don't know the answer. How you position your body as well as certain areas of it conveys about your mental state.

Your posture can show your personality as enthusiastic or friendly, and sad, or even angry or perhaps passionate. If this is so you are in control, it's up for you to utilize it to benefit you.

Avoid assuming postures or gestures that suggest you're unconfident, or anxious. Do not hunch soldiers, fold your back, casting sharp glances towards the ground, gnawing your nails, or even kissing your lips. Do not make the same negative signal repeatedly, such as tapping your soles of your feet against the floor as if you are waiting to see the conversation ended. Don't clench your fists in a snare, rub your teeth or cross your arms around your chest. These could be interpreted as aggression expressions.

People who are able to detect the body language signals don't even interpret it conscious. The brains of these people pick up signals and automatically communicate to them what you're thinking. Therefore, if you don't want to come across as insecure or aggressive, you should keep your back and bend toward your person speaking to you. This shows interest and attentiveness. Utilize your hands to make gestures and then explain your actions as you attempt to impress your audience. Sit up, relax and when appropriate, put on gentle physical gestures to show the level of comfort you have.

Smile and show off your teeth

There is nothing as welcoming like flashing your smile in a smile. If it's genuine the result is the perfect way of telling people you are happy to be with you. One simple smile will lighten your face, and alter your appearance best. The smile of a other person in front of you that you appreciate the way they speak You feel comfortable and comfortable. This is an essential part of your arsenal. It can disarm and entices others for you. There is no need to smile or laugh each time or else it may turn out to be creepy and seem unsincere. But, you should punctuate your conversation by smiling whenever appropriate, particularly when you are trying to make a joke or humorous.

* Talk about everything except your own habits/traits/achievements

Each person has their own achievements Some more so than others, however there is no interest in the place you've been. It could be later, but in the present, when you're just meeting people don't bore them to death by telling them about your accomplishments or the activities you love doing. No! It will cause you to appear confident and self-centered. Save the self-indulgence in the future if they do be seen.

Make sure you don't tell the whole discussion a narrative about your persona or behavior as well. The conversation should be in two directions.

If you let it turn into an argument about traits or accomplishments, both participants will end the discussion feeling exhausted and overwhelmed by the other. You should instead find more exciting topics to discuss in the event that your companion wants to know more about activities you've done or were taking part in. However, you must ensure that you keep your comments to a minimum. There is a chance that you will be found guilty of being boring however, nobody will forgive the pride and arrogance of a bore.

* Don't just listen, but really listen

If you want to be heard by people You must be able to hear. There's a distinct distinction between listening and hearing which most people fail to understand. Everyone can look at you and look at your lips while you talk over the next couple of minutes. However, most people are not aware of the importance of listening their friends and acquaintances they're having conversations with.

The distinction between listening and hearing is in the level of focus you put into the process.

When you are talking, try to be attentive rather than be able to hear the phrases. Keep a close eye on the words you are hearing and the emotion they convey. Being attentive to what you hear could draw someone's attention towards your in a short period of time. It is one of the forgotten arts and becoming a good listener will surely make your friends to hang out with them and chat with them all day long.

Chapter 5: Getting Ready To Speak In Public

In some cases, the difficulty is with public speaking. They are one of the most lively people in the world even when they're just with just a couple of friends, but lack the same brilliance when attending parties or gatherings with many more. If you're one of the individuals in this group this chapter is meant for you. It is designed to make you feel comfortable speaking before audiences that is fifty, five hundred or just five.

* Stop anxiety

There's nothing to worry concerned about when you're scheduled to make public appearances. People aren't going to gobble your flesh. Actually, they're in your corner if you are able to communicate with them. Don't let anxiety hinder your conversation. What's the least that could be the outcome? It's that you lose the conversation however, there are hundreds of more conversations that could be conducted. The points listed below can help you cope in dealing with anxiety.

* Mirror technique

From the beginning of time public speakers have for ages been practicing in mirrors, to provide them with exactly the same experience they'll experience on stage. There is no need to be looking to be an actor or public speaker, however, practicing before the job interview or a date with a romantic partner can make an impact on your performance, since you enter those scenarios well-prepared and pumped.

• Get comfortable with the sound of your own voice

Your voice's sound differs from how you hear inside your head. Make sure to identify the main aspects you want to address and then practice speaking about them in a group. This technique has the same impact similar to the mirror method.

* You improve your skills by experience, not only practicing

As you are immersed in situations where you need to communicate, the better you will become. That's an established fact. Training alone won't make you an excellent speaker or conversationalist. It is time to give up any engagements that demand that you speak for a few phrases to everyone else.

* Don't listen to the inner voice

Everyone has a small uneasy voice that is a part of our heads. It's that voice of worry and a sense of caution, which tries to protect you in a way that keeps you from the spotlight. It's responsible for drawing the attention away and telling youthat "you aren't good enough.. If you don't learn to deflect this voice in certain situations and times, it'll remain an source of your anxiety as it impedes your capacity to engage in positive conversations with people who you interact with often.

Chapter 6: Destroy Your Social Fears And Learn Social Grace

What's the biggest challenge to your capability to influence others in your life, begin conversations with people you don't know, and meet new people easily? Is it the fact that you are not the most physically-attractive person on the planet? Do you struggle with expanding your influence as well as the people you interact often? False answer! Both ways Your biggest fear is something I describe as "the fear of rejection."

Everybody has the same gene. This is a measure of protection created by our minds to act as a safeguard as a brake mechanism that aims to guard us against criticism. But, it could backfire in extreme cases. This could put you in an unwelcome position in which you do not have fundamental social grace, and you find it difficult to engage in the social activities it is your right to do.

If you have trouble to socialize with strangers in a relaxed manner and have successful conversations or developing new relationships with them You are suffering with this anxiety and must get back to building your skills to socialize with ease. The following tips outline what you must look for to improve your social skills.

* Make use of Social verification and verification to your advantage

If you're not socially talented and are not socially adept, you must seek out those who have more in common with yourself when it comes to having the most impressive ability to socialize. Being with a group of friends is a good idea because it has three effects I'm able to see for those who are. You are in less stress than you have in your own home. It's easy to just float during social gatherings like formal dinners or informal gatherings. Additionally, by being a part of with others, you may gain a few points about how to manage discussions. The best teacher is experience so you'll quickly get the hang of it if are able to enlist a wingman or be a wingman for anyone who is knowledgeable. It is also essential to pick confidence. The knowledge that someone will save you in the event that things start to fall apart can put your free to explore. Another benefit is that you could depend on the good name of your acquaintances or friends for a while. In the event that you are in their company they may offer you the benefit of being skeptical, especially if the people in question are famous as a puller.

You can destroy stereotypes from your brain

No! It's not more difficult than talking to gorgeous women, or it is difficult to attract the attention of their admirers. No! The people don't look at you with a sour face because they are small. No! No rule states that you can't meet your partner of life in bars, strip clubs or during a rainstorm when you are heading to the mall. No! There is no reason to not strike an individual you truly would like.

Simply put, there aren't any rules in creating new friendships, except for those you have set for yourself. If you think that gorgeous ladies are more difficult to get to know, you'll find that they're difficult to get to know. If you don't flirt with guys that you enjoy so you can't. It's as easy as it gets. It is essential to dismantle false stereotypes and rules that hold back your social lives. Be in the flow now.

• Learn to offer sincere compliments

Everybody loves honest compliments, people even enjoy flattery that is not genuine. They are a great way to boost our spirits and give us confidence in us. This is a secret that which you must discover.

If every person you're going to get to know is nice so you must give them more. Here's one piece of advice however. Make sure you give only the most genuine compliments.

It's never too late to compliment individuals without getting away from them. Apart from that, unless you're trying to make a point of talking about the great hair they have avoid compliments on the body or switch from "friendly" to "creepy" quickly. Instead, you should compliment the way they look, their fashion sense or something they've said about their accomplishment, or just how you talk to them and smile. Simple compliments about the everyday things in life be more significant.

• Learn how to give praise

Also keep in mind that you should not be so inconsiderate as not to take advantage of compliments that are directed at you. Be open and receptive to any compliments coming to you too. It is your right as well. There are many people who try to find complicated ways to compliments, but often end up messing up poorly. Simply saying "Thank you" is sufficient to most compliments. Recognizing the value of compliments is an important aspect of gaining confidence in social situations too.

* Correct table manners

Food hygiene has been taught to us from the time when we were children; however many people don't have learned them. It is possible that, in the end some people do not bother to learn about them. You ought to not. Making sure you are practicing the proper eating habits is probably the best thing that you can accomplish. If you aren't eating properly in your kitchen it could result in sending a negative impression of table manners to people outside the home. Therefore, make sure this initiative begin at home.

Chapter 7: The Three Golden Rules Of Making New Friends

What are the best practices to make new friends? What can you do to ensure that you're in the right crowd of friends around you? What are the best places to find new people you'll enjoy? This chapter outlines various ways you can remain focused if you would like to make new acquaintances.

One of the questions you must be asking yourself should be "Why should the person I am talking to want to be friends with me?" Or, even better, "How can I make this person want to be my friend?" The question now be aware that you interact with hundreds of people each everyday, many of them would like to become close to you. Would you like to be the same as them all? No! Why?

There is no way to make an acquaintance with every person you want to be your friends as you decide to filter out some. It is only your choice to make friends with those who can help you enjoy fun or meet the goals you set for yourself. Similar rules are applicable to everyone else. Also, you must make sure that you don't be filtered out from other people as well. The reason people are filtered out is many motives. Lack of hygiene, poor manners and timidity, arrogance...the list goes on. It is inevitable that you will be one of the filters for the people that you encounter. How do you make sure you aren't filtered out?

It's simple, really. It is essential to make sure you're providing enough entertainment and value to compensate the personal rules you're violating. If you do that, you'll be forgiven for most other offenses that do not put you on the offence. We will examine these issues closer today.

* Offer value

If you're looking for to have great friendships, you need to be an excellent friend to them you think? Friendship focuses on providing enough worth. Friendships become more enjoyable by sharing similar interests and interests, as well as opinions and opinions regarding life with those who you refer to as your friends.

If you're looking to make friends that increase your productivity, it is important to inquire about the worth you bring to the group.

Are you seeking to build your quality you can offer to your peers? The same way that you assess new applicants to build relationships and friendships and relationships, others look at your worth also. It's definitely easier for you to meet acquaintances when you're an excellent catch. It's much easier to grab your friend's attention when they think they're getting something from the conversation you're having.

* Have fun, be spontanious

Nobody, certainly nobody wants to feel bored. No one will tolerate your being boring. However, even if you and group only talk about current issues regarding eschatology or any more obscure cosmic physics topics but they want that it be as engaging and educational as they can. There are many different definitions of what is fun and so long as you're in the right place in a certain context and setting then you're allowed to continue. Never be labeled "the boring friend." If you're not boring, then you certainly won't be lacking new acquaintances. Some people gyrate at those whom they consider to be fun. Even if they have to accept flaws in their character in the belief that they're most likely to have a good time on a journey along with them. Be a pleasure to spend time with. Use spontaneity in a safe manner Break the limits and rules of the game as you watch others become attracted by your personality.

Mix and mingle with the people who are in the right place.

Are you looking to master the art of public speaking? Begin by hanging out with people interested in the same subject. Are you looking to increase your chess skills? Begin by hanging out with people who have similar interests. In this way, you'll be able to know their colleagues who are fascinated by the same subjects like you. Being a part of the right group is crucial in the quest to create the perfect kind of friendships. Go to places where you're likely to get acquainted with like-minded individuals. It is possible to take an exciting new pastime or passion that lets to meet many more individuals. Try volunteering for community services to meet new individuals. Explore your interests, and make yourself available to events that you're likely to get acquainted with people who share the same interests. This is a method that is never a failure.

Chapter 8: Angry Spouse

You know who the person immediately? You have a clear mental image of the person who doesn't pass through"vibe check "vibe check"? This was me for several years. I was an unhappy spouse. However, truthfully I had sorted out my issues with anger when I got married. You still meet these types of people every everyday. This is how you can tell whether it's yours. It's easy to get angry and are unable to release yourself from small matters. When there's a disagreement that needs to be resolved, it is your responsibility to discover the truth of the matter regardless of what the outcome. Everyone is wrong, minus you. When you're unhappy everyone else is down. Everyone must be aware of their movements about your. Your girlfriend or partner should be watching their words. If they make a sloppy word salad, everything is in a whirlwind. It's the way it is when you have an angry person. Someone who is unable to overcome the situation and takes the time to relax.

The greatest thing about this overall circumstance is that it allows you to be in charge. Before the incident with my dad I was living with my friend. I was just twenty-two years old in the year I lived with her and we were living within Grove City, in the suburbs of Columbus, Ohio. My mother always asked me to purchase her treats when I returned from working. She would often stop by her preferred shop, but the other day, I spotted a location, which was run by an old man. It was an electronics and hardware retailer, which had a large number of men in various sizes, shapes and forms descending into. Every day, I was intrigued by the odd cases of hardware. My usual anger dissipated once I entered the location. The curiosity swept over me and I made my way into the shop. An elderly man explained the youngsters what a microwave does as well as he explained the correct way to repair it. They were absorbing and listening as if they were in awe. The man waved at me after which he took the youngsters out of the shop. I left wondering.

Then, fast forward until the time I dropped my microwave away. However, it did not completely fall apart. After an hysterical riot with my girlfriend and the microwave, I got up and went to the elderly man's grocery store. The zen-like posture of the old man was taking a hot shower for me. And here I am, focused on my anger and anger that I can't even show the extent to which I get. And, there's him, calm, collected, composed. He was looking over the microwave and attempting to repair the problem. Amazingly, he got it fixed. The moment I arrived home, I completely forgot about the whole fight with my friend. I explained everything to her about the man who was old. Her eyes were as if I'd forgotten something.

Through a couple of Google search results, she came across an article that made an impact that was profound on me personally. It was a 20-year long story of a court case against two entrepreneurs. Two of their friends founded an electronic manufacturing firm. A dispute erupted after one of them decided to take the company to himself. He attempted to acquire the business and during the process, he was able to ruin the business by itself. In debt, the selfish co-owner vanished, and another one set up the shop in a tiny space. It all changes towards the right direction after he began to teach young people in the town how to repair and use electronic devices. They were not charged to teach them which made him quite popular among the locals.

Now, he's the CEO of a number of shops which is almost like a franchise that is to say. His motto that has made him very popular was that he has no regrets. He did not let the resentment of losing a rapidly growing business or money take his attention. He remained focused on giving back to the community as well as "manning up," as the man said. He claimed that he didn't think this strategy worked. It was more respectable to be humble even when you fail, rather than pouring water upon everything in a fury. Therefore, whether he was successful or failed was not the issue. Maintaining a positive attitude towards life, refusing to let a negative experience define him in search of growth and wealth is what made him succeed. With that kind of attitude, success won't be at all possible. However, even if he was able to earn the money it wouldn't be considered a success when he was unable to maintain his masculinity. I stared at my phone and realized what type of man I wanted to become. I was not sure of what exactly I was looking for. I knew that I needed something different.

It's the first thing you need to consider. Do you really want to be the violent, angry one you're striving to become? Do you wish to remain your spouse's rage for the rest of your life?

It's not likely. From my own experience and knowing how challenging it can be to control these behaviors and desires. For your benefit it is possible to be more savvy than I was and steer clear of the to the bottom. There is no need to smash an appliance to be in an incredibly life-changing scenario. Instead, you're able to create it.

Consider this question Do you feel great when you're angered? Are you feeling masculine in the face of anger? Are you sure that you wish to link the feelings of masculinity to anger?

I'm hoping that it isn't. Although traditionally, anger and men share a strong bond. From the angry Achilles to the ferocious Mike Tyson, men do like a well-constructed illustration of their anger. It is a biological emotion that humans developed to fight off the predators. When a person saw an animal predator, neurochemical reactions in his brain accelerated and the man was in a position to defeat the predators. These days, however, are gone.

* Today's world, these dangers are not present. In comparison to times in the past, there are none predators. Although, we no longer must fight sabertooth Tigers or bears, we do think of ourselves as men. Consider asking yourself what is manhood for you?

It is taking responsibility to my actions, growing as an improved person, assisting others around me to be more resilient in the face of life's obstacles. It's true that I had no idea that what a man's role means to me immediately. It's not a race but an endurance race. If you want to control your anger it will take more than just one day, or a week and even a full year. The process will require that you change the way you view and think about the world. The concept of manhood isn't a quaint notion that dates back to earlier in time. Middle Ages. It's actually a way of living.

* The reason why male anger management isn't working for the majority of people is because they do not understand it's ultimate aim is. The ultimate goal isn't to squelch anger, rather to recognize that there's another method to live the world. This is where the manhood factor can be found.

Chapter 9: Anger Issues

There's many causes for a person to become angry. The most popular motives include:

* Upbringing

* Family

* Environment

* School

* Job

* Lover

* Spouse

* Friends

* Politics

* Religion

* Celebrities

* Life in general

If you take a look there are a variety of motives to become an angry individual. However, this is only true the case if you let your anger become onto you.

The basic principle of man's anger management is the fact that your anger is the choice of yours. You can choose to let it happen. be in control of. However it's not always easy. There are instances when feeling angry can be completely normal. It could be a sin for you to have no emotion in response to:

* Funerals of loved family members

• Serious career disruption

* Betrayal

* Suffering damage

Life's unexpected twists which turn your entire world about

If you look at these two lists are you able to tell the difference? The list on the first is those that you are able to manage. In other words, you are in the ability to control how you deal with the issues. Another list includes matters that you have no influence on. For example, nobody can control death. A loved person is a very painful moment in the lives of anyone. So, all kinds of responses are common as people are forced to deal with their loss. In addition, they must face loss that they cannot be able to stop at all. However, once the time of mourning has ended individuals mature and grow after loss, and they keep moving forward. They heal their wounds and keep moving forward.

But the feeling of anger towards those at work or in school is something that you are able to take control of. At some point, you will have be able to switch schools and your job and will not encounter those individuals who cause your anger ever again. If you are angry, politicians, celebrities or politicians, is something you control when you let go. If you're not already a politician or famous person, there is a chance that you will instruct Donald Trump a lesson. In fact, you won't get it as the odds of you meeting him are small.

In the end, there are issues that are related to family, or even growing up. The majority of people I've had the pleasure of meeting throughout the years have categorized family as the primary reason to any underlying emotions. The end result is that blaming the entire situation on a time of your life when you didn't feel in control of things is easy. Accepting your faults and confronting your troubles can be a difficult task. Anger issues are an effort to get rid of the anger and establishing your life again instead of engaging in unhealthy behavior for the rest of your life. When we're openly angered by the things on the list above and we allow the destructive behaviors. It appears like we're able to admit our anger in front of us. We have the right to be angry, to express that to others, to break and explode things. Take a moment to think about it.

Manhood? Are you able to imagine historic figures who brilliantly emphasize the idea of screaming at women, or throwing chairs?

I didn't believe it. That's what differentiates weak and strong men and fake men that are truly men. The masculinity of men and their manhood isn't anything to do with the amount of your weight can be lifted. In reality, everything has to do with the ability to manage yourself and show the world your strength, grit and endurance. Being a massive, powerful person who is able to defeat Brock Lesnar, but isn't always there for his family members, is not as good as having a hundred-pound man who's always available for his family. Another one is a genuine man.

The manhood of a man is authentic, as it's not based on any other thing than the foundation of his family and the community. A masculine physique does not mean anything when you consider the actual problems life throws at us. I'm not saying that It's important and great to get fit. But if you are able to take on ten opponents by using your fists but cannot resist the desire to shout at your spouse or mother or your children, then you're not a strong individual. Sure, you're an athlete as well as a martial artist. What about a is that a human being? Not in a moment.

This is because getting angry is simple. It's not difficult in reality. There is no way to mature. Even more than that, you'll wear it as an badge of self-acceptance just like others have to give them to. When someone tries to defy you, or to tell you they are not right You simply label them as enemies. The life you lead is full filled with constant conflict, continuous fights and ever-changing tension. Anywhere you go, people recognize that you're an unpopular person, and they shouldn't be able to relax in your presence. You must have that sort of a ferocious authority respect for the person you are. If not we should prepare ourselves for a single-man performance of city-based Wrestlemania. It's time to take an icy shower. It's the reason why people flee from the person who is.

Chapter 10: Anger And Men

It's not a lie. The story of the business owner deeply affected me. I wanted to take some time and contemplate what I ought to do in the future.

Naturally, I needed to choose. On the one other hand, I could go in the same direction. It is up to me to experience an outburst of anger that could turn my life miserable. It's possible that it won't occur, however anyone can be affected by those who are angry. A small puddle of stench slowly entered me. I heard whispers and shushing. Another way was available. When I was younger I did not know that what it would be like. I'd eventually refer to as manhood. There wasn't a term for it in the moment. There was a feeling that was telling me there was a different method.

At this point, when most teenagers break. They wish to remove the anger in their lives. But the issue isn't with the discipline aspect, but rather in the search for a suitable alternative to anger.

The girl I was with left shortly after. I was 23 in the moment We were staying in Grove City. My normal method of handling heartbreak and breakups was to blast out. Slaves, plates or furniture over, or general damage to things, call it what you want... It's happened to me. tried the whole lot. Screaming, shouting, and even being violent are things I'm prone to. But, what I am grateful for is that I've never struck women. However, this doesn't make my previous mistakes any less savage. In the past I was an extremely dangerous person. After my girlfriend announced to me she was going to leave me, I knew immediately the reason. I shut my eyes, and saw that black, growing intense feeling. Inducing me to explode to shout, and to smash the things I own, and get back my share of what's mine. I got up off the seat and saw her shaking. There was a crack in my body. I realized that she did not possess the means to combat me physically or verbally. Most importantly, I could feel her anxiety. In watching her flinch in terror I knew that she was struggling to make this choice for some time. One of the most difficult aspects of that fight was how she'd have the courage to share the information to me. In the present, it was one of the least sexiest breakups that I've had to endure in my entire life. We talked for one hour. She shared all the things she did not like about me. I took a seat and listened. When she was done the conversation, I thanked her for her honesty, then I let her go and go. It was a strange feeling, but I was sad and heartbroken simultaneously. I lost the person I've always loved. But, I overcame my anger.

The first time in my entire life, I put the anger to rest. I refused to let it control my life. Now I'm the boss. I'm the one in charge and not the rage. What was new this time?

In this case, I was not going to let my anger control me. The thing I wanted most was to control my anger. The idea that you aren't able to handle how you feel is the primary reason why you aren't able to enhance your situation. You believe that there is a divine force behind to feel rage is the primary reason for the entitlement you feel. In reality it's you who are the only control of your actions. It is your responsibility to decide on whether you'll blast or not. The reasons behind anger could be from the external side. However, how your response to them will be completely your choice. You are sure likely to be angry and everyone else will at the end. Anger is an entirely natural human emotion.

The distinction that separates true men from pretentious, entitled guys is their capacity to stop their desire to satisfy. Be it alcohol, drugs or gambling or the desire to be angry, men are judged by their capacity to resist the temptation. The day I stood up to the anger in my heart and rage, I was going on a voyage. The thing I did not know was that this was my journey toward becoming a man. True, my biological makeup fulfilled every requirement to qualify as an adult male. In my opinion, I was still an self-centered boy. But, things changed the day.

I reacted to her in a way that was honest. Sure, I was not a good partner. My anger was always the first priority and negative thoughts over my love for her. I was a yeller at her numerous times, more often than I recall. When anything occurred that put me a bit outside my comfort zone, I'd yell. I have never offered an ear to her issues or opinions. I'm not surprised she quit me.

It was still a bit angry. However, it appeared to disappear faster than it usually does. My heart was hurting however, I was on an obligation now. I was looking to transform. The most important thing of any other factor was the fact that I could control my anger. In the room, my first step in my recuperation took place. I discovered that no matter your anger or circumstance, it is possible to be a good friend to your self. In fact, it is possible to prevent yourself from doing a mistake that could be fatal. The most dangerous and greatest thing concerning masculine anger control is that everything depends on your ability to be able to say no. If you're unable to be honest with yourself and then instill the same sort of discipline then you'll never be able to make it.

Manhood isn't something that you can do one time and then your life gets better. In fact, being a man is something you strive for all the time, each day of the week, every month in the same week throughout the year, up to end your life. It's why being unhappy and engaging with negative behaviors is simple. You don't need any dedication and you're all it takes. Manhood, however, takes real dedication.

The next night, I climbed into the bed easily. My head was clear and my thoughts were clear. I had no idea that an enormous shift was already happening. All I knew was that the world was about to alter. For the first time in my life, things were about to improve.

Chapter 11: Anger And Forgiveness

Someone who has been afflicted with anguish for many years may think twice about this idea. The truth is, the idea is being proposed here is basically a plain traditional "let it go." But, it sounds so simple.

If you've been thinking about this same line, then congratulations. That's so easy. No one gets up and declares that they will never be irritable ever again. It would be fantastic to have that happen. But, most of the time, it doesn't. In reality, individuals require an effective catalyst. Usually, it comes through the experience of a life-changing event. The moment when their anger has a result that they are unable to change. The consequences of this can cause a lot of hurt and separation from close friends, ruin relationships, turn off lovers and spouses etc. One may be forced to realize that the way they conduct themselves can be the reason the situation is in place and they are responsible to alter their behavior. The question of whether or not they'll be able to change their behavior is dependent on the ability they have to say no to their right to anger.

The situation can get difficult. One might ask, reasonable in order to show that their rage is deep-seated. This isn't because they're angry at the government or even a famous person. Their anger however, they say is different from the other types of anger. It's the result of memories, unsolved emotions, or even trauma. In the majority of cases the anger is a result of their personal group of family members, friends or even acquaintances. If someone is struggling in this way it is because they think that the person who is in the conflict is owed something. They want an opportunity to shift the scales, or to find an avenue to maintain the friendship. But, they would like to make it happen on their conditions. That means the person who is at the root of the anger needs to recognize their own feelings and point of view, alter their behavior into a an appropriate way for our needs. That's why it's almost impossible to see this happen in the real world.

Be aware that people have a selfish nature. Like you and me everyone has different motives and motivations to act how they behave. How you deal with issues is similar to how you deal with yours. If you do not have some kind or special connection that you are able to count on anyone else to make things the right choice for you. It's completely illegitimate and childish to believe that people take more interest in your emotions rather than their own. If you're looking to make a change then this is the initial assumption about someone you have to release. I am more aware than anybody else. When my ex-girlfriend quit me, I was left with plenty of time to think. Once my work was completed I'd go back home to lay on my sofa. While I was going through my mobile phone's address book, discovered the names of my people who I had left out throughout my lifetime. Certain people ended their relationships with me and I broke up with a lot of them. When I was arguing with people I've never asked me the question: Do the people who are arguing with me really have a problem?

No They don't. If you consider it, it's really not insane. In fact, I've had never thought about whether I was a fan of the actions of those involved, or even why they acted the way they did. The thing I wanted most was for them to be able to address the accusations I made. I didn't care about how people were feeling or the reason they felt such a in that way. I just focused on myself.

There I was, standing at the point of no return. It is now clear that I needed to combat my anger. What can I do even if the cause of my anger has always been present? How do I get rid of my anger when there always was a reason to feel angered?

My head would hurt for many days. However hard I tried, I just couldn't release the frustration. I tried looking things in a different point of viewpoint, but it was to the point of no return. There was a myriad of options to prove my fiction and make the other person look less bad than I did. But what I was really struggling over was this notion that I must never allow myself to be the one who is responsible. The other party that is at fault. That's, at least, the only method to keep my appearance clear in any situation.

But the issue was that the thought process didn't reduce my anger it was more of an excuse to rationalize my anger. I tried, and tried to release it but couldn't. When I started to ask myself what was the reason? I was pondering why it is so difficult to forgiving?

The million-dollar issue, and the response was not surprisingly straightforward. One of the reasons I was unable to forgive people was that I was trapped in anger. If I could just get rid of my anger, what else would remain? When I looked inward I realized that anger was the primary emotion. What I did, and everything I believed, had to do to that feeling. It was all like a B-rated film which urged me as the principal persona, to explode at other people. It hit me. It would have been a complete loss were it not for my anger. My anger has been an influencing factor throughout my life. It was so powerful, so influential it was that I wasn't sure what I was supposed to do with it. It was like I didn't be able to think or do anything without it. It was there trying to rid myself of the feeling.

If you're like the majority of you who are reading this you're in a pivotal time. In this article, I'll give you the secrets to:

• Get rid of all your rage

Be a more healthy person

* Find many more acquaintances

Create a more positive connection with your partner or partner

* Live a more fulfilling life with your family

Enjoy a happier social life

You can become a person magnet

The problem, however, lies in the next. The first step is to be able to forgive. The first person to forgive is you. It might sound odd. As an angry individual, you've likely caused enough damage to someone else. However, when you begin taking a closer look at your relationships to other people and realize that there's plenty of people that you should not forget. If you apply the basic principles to understand this, in order before you can move on with your new direction it is necessary to accept their forgiveness regardless.

The key is to comprehend the scientific basis behind anger. Based on the APA the APA, anger is a feeling which is activated when your brain senses threats. It sends a signal to the region of the brain known as the amygdala. This increases the amount of the level of adrenaline within our bodies. So anger is a natural human response. The process of controlling it, however, is more difficult than this. Another APA research also shows that individuals can control their anger. You don't need expensive medication to do so. Instead, it's a matter of training yourself to handle the anger. It was a component of my research into cognitive restructuring. This is an idea that's based on cognitive psychology, which employs a variety of techniques like thought recording, Socratic questioning, or guided imagery. According to research in a number of research studies conducted by Darin Dougherty who is an HMS assistant professor of psychiatry in the Massachusetts General Hospital, there are more sophisticated research studies, such as those in the Alien Therapy game. The game lets kids kill animated aliens as they avoid snails. Children must be taught to regulate their urges. This is what they have done. If they're able do it, then you can too.

When it's the time to consider taking that decision into consideration, it's going be a lot tougher. Thinking about one incident which happened a long time ago doesn't make sense. The majority of folks have already forgot about the event. The only thing that's left is you constantly thinking about it so you must forgive them. It's the same as forgiving yourself. Release them and become liberated. It's not the same when dealing with the people to whom you caused harm. The situation gets even worse in the event that you find out you have hurt people. Even though resolving to forgive others can be one tough ride but asking forgiveness for yourself is completely different. It doesn't matter how you respond, only the degree to which others be willing to accept the apology. This is where the cycle of forgiveness starts. Every day, you'll have to fight these decisions. Sounds hellish? You can be sure it's. In this article, I'll help you make your life a more simple. I'm going share an idea to you.

Simply, release it. Try using this trick, which worked for my experience. In my time of anger, I'd caused a number of injuries to people. From those who chose to avoid me, to those who were afraid of me. I'm sure there's many people who did not want me to be to be in their space. Of course, there are those that did have a right to be exiled from the world for their conduct in regard to me. However, the majority of individuals who hurt me did not merit such harsh punishment. As I reread all of their actions, I realized that their actions weren't true. They weren't real enough for me to eject them from my life completely, yet I did what I could to make it happen. The worst part was as I realized how much harm I did to my time in life. It was like getting up to find my feet stuck in the concrete of a block. It was impossible to move and I was unsure of the best way to move. It was a blessing that I had kind of"aha" moment. I made the choice to "make the slate clean" to start over. Because I am unable to change what was already happening as well as I'm only able to accept the forgiveness of those who have done harm for me, then why don't be able to let myself go from my unforgivable mistakes from the past? They weren't inexplicably wrong. I wasn't able to kill someone or steal a bank. However, as I was a person with my own opinions and beliefs and beliefs, others did too. If they aren't ever letting me down, then it's fine. Yet, I free myself from the binds of sorrow and frustration. No matter what happens, I am sure that this meeting will not turn to an all-out conflict. In fact, it's likely that there will be no outcome. The only thing that is, or ever has been only the thing that is seen to be seen by man. It's that's all there is of it.

Chapter 12: Male Anger Management

Then, here's the deal... we're going to reveal the most important secret. There is a method to get rid of the frustration and maintain the masculinity. It's possible to improve your self-esteem and overcome the traits that can ruin your existence and rob you of your pleasure. This isn't the use of hypnosis or transformative karmic process. This is a phenomenon that's been going on for a long time. It's been called many things that have caused confusion to individuals looking to address their anger problems. That's Male Anger Management.

Are you feeling cheated? Do you feel like it was sitting around waiting for you to grab it? Now let me ask this question: Why didn't you?

If you're sincere and honest, you'll realize that's the entire point. For one second. The main purpose is to figure out an avenue to stop being annoyed all the time. This is a simple answer but it is a bit difficult due to its simple. To improve your character and grow into an improved person, you must be able to control your anger. It means you acknowledge that there is no excuse for your actions. You and only you will be accountable for your actions to the consequences of your actions, and if anything takes place, nobody is responsible but yourself. If you don't alter your identity, the question is who else will?

But it's definitely not as if you're fighting the way of Gandhi. He is the perfect example of the issues we're talking about in this article. In the face of foreign troops in India acting as they pleased, Gandhi looked for a method to defeat them. He was aware that he could not fight the invaders using arms and so sought an alternative method. The nonviolent way of protesting and performing required to put oneself in danger but stay with his posture and manner of conduct. The conviction he held was more powerful than the gun. This is why everybody recognizes his name but isn't able to remember the invaders in any way. The purpose of letting go the anger is to develop the character of a person who is greater than anger. The work you do is yours. You must do this on your own.

It might seem a little bleak. You're likely be making a number of sacrifices in order in order to attain this kind of quality of character. The Bible declares "thou who ask shall receive," and the universe, in all its glory can send something direction. As I made the transition from man to woman I tried picking new activities. The hobby wasn't something major I was just playing around trying to keep my mind busy. A few days ago, I walked into the grocery store to purchase an Ice cream. At the time, I was 25 when I went to Pittsburg for work. job. It was a scorching day and I was in need of something to cool down. When I left the grocery store, I witnessed the hand of a stranger fly directly across my face. The person who slapped me fell on my ice cream. I could feel my pent-up anger boil into a roar of absolute fury. I was able to convince my to refrain from doing so. While I was about unleash a volley of insults at the person I spotted that it was a woman. The way she looked, her beautiful eyes filled with admiration instantly. It was as if someone had put cold water over my head. It was a split second which forced me to decide. The first moment in my life I smacked a smile onto my face, got up, washed myself and I introduced myself to the woman. The conversation was awkward, and she demanded for coffee for apology. We exchanged numbers, and then set the date of our next meeting. Then, boom. I was the winner, and it was my prize. In the end, I discovered that the lady didn't win deliberately. The incident was just a mishap with. It was the first ever in my life, I was ecstatic when I was hit by someone.

Then, I decided to say"no" to myself. One thing distinct from before was the motive behind this "no". I wasn't sure that shouting at a woman about the ice cream taste was worthy of my time. I wanted to make improvements in my situation, right?

If I did be able to yell at a woman in a manner such as that, it'd immediately confirm my character. That's why I decided not to become that kind of person again. These relationships that ended friendships have taught me a lesson. I was not a person magnet and that's the kind of person I'd like to be. It's quite easy. If I could not change into this person, and handle my anger I'd never develop and enhance my life. This is why saying "no" is so expensive. That means you'll have strive to become a man through saying no to getting annoyed. In the beginning, it was clear to me that a real man isn't one to yell at his woman. This is a fact that's non-negotiable. We never even consider it, think about it or revisit the issue. Forget about the ice cream, it's time to buy a new one. However, if you make the situation easier for a woman or for anyone else, in general, tells much about your character.

This makes you attractive. You have proven that you're more mature than others. You go about your day with at ease and are not bothered about the smallest issues. You are tall and display your ferocity when faced with a challenge. In the end, you will be able to rest comfortably around you as they are convinced that you've got the coolest of heads. As soon as they meet you they will feel that they can speak with you and rely on your. They are able to tell because your appearance reflects maturity and manhood. You are able to manage yourself as an adult. Your character and principles are your main assets. In search of that quality and character as well as insisting on always defending them, brought me to the most memorable moment in my life. If I had yelled at her that day, and let the slightest bit of anger go out, I wouldn't had met my wife.

Chapter 13: Life, Character, Principles

I could not think about the woman. When you live, when the time for marriage is when you take a look at someone and tell them, "yeah this is it!" I felt the same sensation. There was a rogue thing lurking at me from the shadows, gnawing off my bliss.

I was eager to get her in touch but was unsure of what I wanted to tell her or what to say about me. I saw her that day and she didn't know anything about my background. She also didn't understand much about the transformation I was experiencing. Gradually, I paid off the majority of my loans, got an employment opportunity, and then moved into a brand new residence. My life began to run just like clockwork. It was like someone had entered cheat codes into an online game. It was like my life. Everyday, I did increasing my efforts. I was more determined to hit home runs, and hit the hits. I was able to score where it mattered. Only difference was that I decided to adhere to the manhood principle as a matter of course. It is the greatest and the most holy of my principles I follow in my everyday existence. After much reflection I realized that anger was a factor that could have destroyed my character. This was the biggest weakness of my. It's the reason I changed into one of my strongest strengths.

There is a reason to dress male-like in the first instance? What's the deal, you ask? What's the reason you'd need to display your male majesty?

It's been used as a ideal of men over the centuries and even millennia. It doesn't matter how large or little, every society has myths and stories concerning the manhood of men. These stories revolve around people who are known for their morals and their knowledge regarding the globe. It is their character, beliefs, and their view of the world that drives people to do things that which others can't. The reason why they are able to is the same principle. Manhood is not about the amount of the weight you are able to lift however, it's about how much you care about the poor and the way you live up to an ethical code of behavior. Like I said before anger is extremely simple. Insisting to grow is a challenge yet it's the hallmark of manhood. The people who act and think such a way that they alter the course of history, and are regarded as outstanding humans.

I was preparing to go on the date. It wasn't actually an actual date, but I'm sure you're getting the idea. My enthusiasm was unbelievable. However, I wasn't really having an action strategy. In the past, I hadn't ever thought about what I was supposed to do with women. The only thing I thought about was an instinct. It was time to present my self in the most positive image I could. The time was running out and I needed to leave. My brain went to sleep during the trip to the venue. Traffic flowed effortlessly as did I when I was nearing my destination. The first night was nothing significant. The first time we met, it was over a beer and then drinking a couple of more times in much less time. It's like a kid-like youthful feeling to hang around. There's no doubt about it today... yes, was I having fun the night I was there.

The ingrained notions of the way to sexually win and end your day in a specific way, ended up being completely unimportant. We're here, together with her. One thing that makes me feel at ease is simply the realization that my view or attitude that night will not be affected, no matter the outcome. What she thinks of me was an obnoxious or unpleasant person was not an issue. I'll take it to the side and move to the next. I had a blast, and she also had hers. When the night came to an end, I had my personal life, my values and my personality to care for. It was my decision not to be weighed down by trivial issues. Manhood for me is built around the concept that I am growing and also proving that I am worthy of my own self by being able to adhere to the rules and principles I set for me. Rules were chosen by myself. If I had not abided by these guidelines or principles that I have set, I'd be doing any harm except to me. The purpose behind man's character and the human nature in general is to provide you with a the chance to realize your dream to life. The only way to achieve that will what you want to be truly achievable.

It was a good time to revisit the date.I was just discussing life. The girl moved to my town just a couple of months ago. Every now and then we dug our feet into the murky water of previous relationships. After our third drink the woman said she'd like to find people who resembled me. I was shocked by her comment. made her bite her lip as she thought she was saying too much. However, we finished the drinks, and headed to bed. After the evening, she embraced me. It was as if someone pressed the button that sent me straight into Pluto. There was nothing physically different in me, but I was in a brand new space.

It was an exhilarating journey to home. I could not sleep due to the joy. It's been two years from the breakup that I blogged about. It took me 2 years to decide on the new relationship. It was the hardest two times in my life. I would have to deception to say that the things I've completed. It was to say that you're doing this. After that, the anger dissipated and the character grew from the fiery carcass of anger. Although, this is more like an episode from the Rick and Morty show than a real actual situation. It's true. To get rid of anger and keep your sexiness requires commitment. The only way to make yourself better than the anger you have is to make a commitment to the more positive things in your the world. For now, each to his own. Eliminating my anger was probably the greatest problem I faced. Perhaps you're dealing with a different issue. However, come what it is, the sole solution to the issue is to take a decision to do another solution. Most likely, it will solve the root cause of the issue.

The most effective way to accomplish it is to dedicate yourself to establishing character. Being a good person is the best symbol of masculinity. This is because to be a true man is about saying "no" to the unhealthy desires. Furthermore that we can overcome those needs, the newly developed personality gives us a fresh opportunity to live. As we no longer suffer from the issues that we faced, we are able to focus in achieving our new objectives. The focus of our goals should be on the improvement of our lives is vital. This is the best way to overcome the turmoil and reach menhood. It's impossible to expect anything to change in the absence of attempting to alter it. If we are willing to make changes and are actively working toward it, can change be achievable. This is why there's no magic solution to our issues. It is essential to demonstrate a genuine determination to solve the problem for us to be able to solve the issue.

Then, there's only one method to completely let go of the anger. It is essential to get rid of the anger. It's my experience. I'm sure you're feeling an emotion that no one is able to comprehend. This is what makes you perform actions that you're regretting. No matter the number of occasions you feed the animal, there's not enough. The animal always demands more. It will always want more, up until the moment when you begin the idea of a new food regimen. The diet will improve your life.

Chapter 14: Achieving Manhood

Manhood is the ultimate degree of self-development. If there's a point at which the most complete realization a man is capable of, it's manhood. You can become that person who you've always wanted to be.

The idea behind it is quite straightforward. The idea is that you will develop different habits and patterns of thinking which can serve as an alternative to anger. Your character and values will help you to follow the proper direction. The first thing you need to do is discover your principles of guiding. Be assured that it's not necessary to learn Ethics 101 at a local university. Choose the people or people whom you respect. If reading is what you like and you're looking for a book, go to your local library or look through the books available on Amazon for a book which is suitable for your preferences. Be aware that everyone is unique and to each their own. There are many different people with diverse background and experiences. When two men experience an anger issue, they will experience the same emotions in two distinct ways. That's why this is your experience. Take it in the same way as you would a journey.

Once you've looked through books, pages hyperlinks, and other others, it's time to work on your masculinity. One of the first things you need to accomplish is to pinpoint your areas of pain. There is no need write them down as long as it is helpful to you. Simply ensure that you have the thoughts on your mind. It doesn't mean you must to dwell on them. simply keep them in your the back of your mind. What you must be considering is the way you'll be able to keep your beliefs in check. Principles are the most important instrument you'll need to use to overcome the anger. The principles while important as they might be, are not the main focus of your tale. The most important thing you should spend time on is how you conduct your own behavior. There are many educated people who are shady, evil or evil and miserable. The knowledge, regardless of how amazing it may be, will remain worthless if left to an unjust man. Yes, you could search "ethical quotes" or "motivational quotes" but it will not give you a moral or a motivational. The concept of managing anger places you in a superior situation to become your self-governing supreme authority. This can only be done by taking responsibility. The ability to be accountable to your actions is an essential part of human character.

Manhood occurs when you make the decision to hold yourself accountable. A responsible man does not allow him to get angry at other people, since he is aware that he is accountable to him first, before any other person. He does not require an external authority to validate his bad behavior. He's the only source of validation, guided by the fundamentals. He doesn't search at the repercussions of bad conduct. In fact, a man who becomes a man is driven by the desire to apply his values and character throughout his daily life. There is no limit to the number of sessions or seminars you attend. There's no need to count what books you've go through or the self-help experts you are listening to. If you don't discover a way to apply these concepts into your own life. This alone will be too difficult to most people. The concept of manhood but, has been that has been practiced for centuries. It's not necessary to take for a five or four-figure program to master something. You're the best person you can ever be. Get yourself involved.

This is the guideline to achieve success. Try to emulate these behavior and behaviors until you feel the sense of being a man becomes normal to you. This is all there is to it. The next step is the most difficult. The trick is to complete it.

First thing you need be doing is kick off the deadline on this adventure. No matter how other people are doing it, what matters is the length of time you have to complete it. In the end, don't make yourself do it. The change is only beneficial in the context of being easy to do so. You can try to make yourself do it however it will not have any impact. In this case, it's not about what you're aware of about mens' roles, but when you embody the concept and practice the way you want to live it. This is not only for occasions, but throughout your daily routine. Treat each day as an individual adventure And leave the track of manhood behind it. The thing you should be doing is insist on the discipline of your daily routine. In addition being open to contemplative thoughts. You should be able to think about whether you really need to be upset. Be open about your reflection also. It isn't necessary to divulge your findings or ideas with any other person. Simply be open to yourself. If you've made a mistake, confess it and then change your behavior.

The concept of manhood, when it's authentic it can be seen in a matter of minutes. The man can be a character or figure out other ways to display your masculinity, but it's not possible to perform it all the time. The act you put on isn't for the rest of time. Even if, however, you are facing issues right now, and are willing to face the issues you face, you'll earn recognition. The people around you will appreciate and support the changes you've made and the struggles as they will see you're doing it for the right reasons. Every person has difficulties and struggles of their own. What people don't want to be around is anyone who is more difficult than their own. The people don't require you to be perfect. There is no such thing as perfect. What people loathe the most is other people who make their troubles seem like the biggest issues around the globe. The majority of people would like people close to them to be better over them. They require for them to be like that because they are hoping that the problems they face can be solved. You can ask yourself this. If you're going to a long-distance trip for the year, and can only bring one person. It is possible to choose two individuals. The one is constantly trying to appear their best as well as be optimistic and has a positive outlook towards life. One is constantly unsatisfied, does not look the best, and is always trying to make everyone feel bad to everyone around their own. Who do you pick?

The chances are that you'll choose with the first one. It's a no choice. You'll choose to do it since you're not able to imagine suffering all year long with an individual who is qualified to improve. You're looking for someone who that you can trust and who will be a smile even in risk, and isn't ever going to let go of the ideals he has set for himself. Being a man makes you this type of person. If you are unsure, admit it and place yourself in a place to decide. Try to think about the possibility that the possibility of being taken to a long-distance trip for the duration of the year. You don't want to skip having fun right currently. You can be the first one to pick.

Chapter 15: Maintaining Manhood

You're now on the road to becoming a man. After a few months it, you begin to question every aspect of your life. It is tempting to throw out the whole thing, and say that it's what it's about. But, even though you struggle with the desire to be successful. But how do you persevere?

It's the most important point in the whole book. If you're not able to summon the determination to continue towards manhood You'll never be able to make it. It might sound evident, but this is what you're doing. The entire point of being a man is to be something that you decide to stand for freely. It's a fact manhood is dependent upon your desire to achieve it. There's no guru or master, there is any self-help instructor, and nothing. You and only the determination to be successful. Apart from the two, you're all that's needed.

It was the best lesson my wife has ever taught me. After some wonderful years of romance I got married. I was thirty in the year I got married and our first year was akin to an Hollywood love story. We had a great time, were positive about the future and she was able to envision the remainder of her life together. In my mind I wondered how long I could hold the relationship going. It was all I had promised in the book. But I came to a halt at the end of a year in my marriage. Manhood began to wear me out. I didn't feel any anger, just the sense of it being a little more intense in the course of the time. There was a feeling of anger every now and then. The anger was minor in comparison to the previous years but, most important my wife had never seen my anger as the man I was prior to meeting her. The question popped up immediately before me. Do I go back to my old habits which could mean losing my love for the person I have always loved Do I just keep going?

The reason was simple. It was impossible to lose her because of an issue as silly as the having the right to be an adult male. The woman I was with cared for I was loved, cherished me and was determined to deliver to my kids. I was wise enough to not allow her to blame me for my bad behaviour. However, I needed to remain realistic. I needed to come up with the way to overcome.

One thing I learned immediately was that having no external motivator isn't enough. In other words, when I had gone through the changes I had a lovely wife, wonderful friends and even had restored my connection to my parents. Thus, being able to keep the relationships was plenty in terms of motivation. It wasn't enough, however, for me. Being worried about losing it all and having to start over was more stressful than it already was. It was a huge burden. If I could keep on working to become man and further refine my masculinity?

Was it possible to have any purpose, or if there was no need to rush? Instead, manhood is an attitude to living, and the way you handle your own life and conduct yourself?

This would mean I was actually in constant necessity to make myself better. To become a better man and to grow more powerful. to be more tolerant as well as to establish myself as the leader of my family and be a man that people like and naturally seek out them. In reality, the one thing that keeps me better existence is what every human being is entitled to. Do your best to achieve it. Win.

from happiness in the arms of my beloved wife and next children is me. Since that first day at the store until today I have been, and am still the sole one who has stopped me from being happy. As I reflect on it, there's only me who is scared of screaming towards my wife. This is my wife after all. The only person who can possibly shout at her is none except me. So, why should I allow myself to go and ruin my family, my marriage for the sake of satisfying such needs?

It's not fair. Then I got to the other room and was able to hug my wife. I nearly cried in that time, and she realized there was something wrong. The years passed and it was only just recently, I told her the whole story. She encouraged me to publish this book so that I could assist young men struggling the same way as I did. There's no way to transform you into a better person or make you a more pleasant person. Only if that you desire with all your soul and heart. It boils down to the extent to which you truly would like this. If you really want it you should go out and purchase it. For no one will ever stop you from being the most perfect version of you and become a man.

All it boils down to is your decision on whether or not you'd like to make a change. If you're looking to make a change then you'll realize that it will be extremely difficult to make the change. It'll take period of time, but the end result will be well worth the effort. As you grow your life, you'll see how your world changes. You'll see many new opportunities for you and people all around you. As you grow and gaining experience, you will not lose the people or opportunities as the way you were before. Genuineness will be evident and illuminate the way in front of you. All you do is filled with the new energy of. That's the nature of masculinity.

It's true, and this is how it has worked for me. It wasn't all the same time. Actually, it was a slow process that took many years to complete.

The rewards, however, are real and I'm happy for these. The only thing that was needed was one only one "no" when it mattered the most. It was a singular "no." Saying no to entitlements is the only thing that counts over the long haul.

There's just one issue to be discussed. What do you plan to do? Are you going to stick with the same old habits? It is not my wish. Take advantage of the things you're entitled to. Trust me, a

Chapter 16: What Is Value

The term "value" refers to everything you do to resolve a issue or enhance someone's quality of life. The term can be interpreted as something you can give as a gift in exchange for money. Value goes beyond the ability to solve issues, so let's declare that value refers to something that is worth it. Give value as there isn't a single value to solve problems thus, it is important to find value.

In the context of these definitions, it is a fact that in order for something to be considered worth it, it needs to either resolve problems or benefit an individual's life, and we can also observe that value is a source of cash.

A lot of times, you'd like to know the reason why someone works for hours because of a single sheet or material

(Money)? Two papers might be worth different amounts because of the numbers printed on them. What's the distinction between the numbers #500 and 200 (Nigerian Currency) is it due to the pictures that appears on their backs? If so, this means that the value of Dr. Nnamdi Azikiwe is $500 as is the worth is of Alhaji Sir. Ahmadu Bello is 200, however, in reality both of them are worth more than that. All my illustrations are just meant to help clear that it's not about the form of the texture, color image, or even what's written on a coin which gives it value, not worth.

Value may also be defined in a simple way as a connection between the perceived benefits and cost perception Value = Benefits/Cost.

Some people consider value to be an intelligence state of mind. To others, values are an essential element of the human experience and play a significant part in how you live your life.

One of my mentors Christ Ani said "Don't just collect, be an effective value-giver (In every form).

Fela Durotoye has once stated, during an interviews in the company of The Catalyst (Lanre Olusola) He said that we are two types of people around the globe;

1) O God-man: O God-Man! It is the kind of man that other do not pray for to surround their lives, as when they meet, when they are aware of your presence the only thing they can say (O God) (O God) because they realize that the presence of you in that gathering won't bring solution to their problems and instead create the situation become

more complicated for them. That's why you're not an individual of any value.

But the man of this type is always welcomed in any event, even if you do not intend to attend and they'll call them because they are confident that you'll provide an answer to what's happening, which means you're a man with worth. "Try not to become a man of success. Rather become a man of value". Albert Einstein The big question right now is what kind of person are you? Knowing the value of what we have can help us focus our minds about how to become important.

Chapter 17: How To Become Valuable

"Good values are like a magnet - they attract good people." John Wooden

1.) Explore your dream

2.) Keep your faith in the positive

3.) consider failure to be a success

4.) Create opportunities and maximize your profits

5.) Always learn and keep in your pursuit of knowledge

6.) Be aware of how you can handle your wants and needs

7) Find solutions to the problems

8) Think and Rethink

9) Set goals

10.) Time Management & Conversion

11) Live A Lifestyle You Can Afford

1. DISCOVER YOUR VISION

One aspect that makes is unique to people is the ability to see their dreams early. Take a look at every famous and successful individual in the world who discovered their vision early on throughout their lives.

Are you aware you know that Bill Gates started coding at the age of twelve?

Elon musk was studying Encyclopedia Britannica by 4th grade At the age of 12, He earned $500 from selling a computer game made by him.

Michael Dell of Dell computers became the first CEO of Dell company.

when he was at the age of 19.

Michael Jordan started baskbasketballage 7

Take a look at these individuals who have been champions in their respective fields. "early to rise is early to shine"

Are you able to see your eyesight? If not, why do you have to be waiting for?

for?

If you're not aware, a vision is an image of the ideal future. If you've not been able to identify it It's time to get it. It's true that your eyes are a part of you, waiting for your discoveries.

How can you find your purpose?

a. Take note of the things that captivate you

b. Be aware of the voice in your head.

C. What you do is can be a compass to help you see.

A clear and focused vision can enable you to be successful.

2). BE POSITIVE

"A positive outlook is essential for being valuable"-Bukola Sunday

When you are doing anything that you wish to accomplish by having a positive attitude to it can lead you to the chance to succeed by 80%. This is due to the fact that you believe that you can succeed in doing what you wish to achieve, and believing that it is possible to devote all of your energy and energy into the goal.

"Fortune sides with him who dares." -- Virgil

When you're positive, be sure to stay clear of

People who are negative, what is the reason?

Seven things that negative people can cause you to suffer. They'll...

1. Make sure you are able to show your worth;

2. Disrupt your photo

3. Drive you crazy!

4. Let your dreams go. You can discredit your imagination!

6. Frame your skills and

7. Don't believe in your own opinions!

Beware of those who are negative!

"Good things happen in your life when you surround yourself with positive people." -Roy T. Bennett

Imagine that you would like to be a chartered accountant. You think that once you've graduated there is no way to get work even though other people are working, but with this mindset of doubt, you'll never be a graduate and talk about your getting a job since you don't know your goals and that could affect how much your time and effort you invest.

In the subject you're doing your research.

"You need to have faith in yourself. Be brave and take risks. You don't have to have it all figured out to move forward." -Roy T. Bennett

If Bill Gate along with the other gatekeepers do not have a positive outlook, are you sure they'll get the respect they deserve in today's community?

In order to be important, you must be positive about whatever you

You might like to explore.

"What's holding you back from becoming wealthy? The majority of times the answer is simply an inability to believe. If you want to become wealthy it is essential to believe that you're capable of doing it and do the things required to reach your goals." Suze Orman

2). Learn And Keep Learning

"The most appealing thing about learning is that no one can ever take it away.

From the people who love you." From you." B.B. King

"The day you stop learning, you start dying. It must be a continuous process for you to become more valuable"Bukola Sunday. Bukola Sunday.

What is it that you learn? It is the act of acquiring or try to gain the knowledge or ability to accomplish things. Also, it means attending an educational course or exercise or to learn of a negative experience in order in order to learn and improve from mistakes made. It is also a way of learning (To learn how to know; be aware of what's happening; and to discover)

."An investing in knowledge will pay the highest dividend." Benjamin

Franklin

There is a saying that readers have the potential to be leaders. This is because once you acquire the information you need, you'll be comfortable to be any place and speak in groups and appear to be someone who is valuable because you be a positive influence on things. When that you don't learn, you end up dying, so you must keep in your learning process if you'd like to stay relevant and brimming with a lot of worth.

"The more you learn, the more you earn." Frank Clark

Check if you're not eager to study and want to be famous or make money and I am sorry to declare you a fool or maybe you're not prepared to learn.

This is the time to think about these questions.

How many novels have you recently read through this time of the pandemic?

What are the most important things I learned thus far?

"Rich people have small TVs and big libraries, and poor people have small libraries and big TVs." Zig Ziglar

Do you wish to emerge out of the pandemic in the same manner you went into it?

If you are have been reading this publication after the COVID 19's pandemic you

Are I gaining knowledge?

* What do I need to be learning?

Do not think that you have everything, study to unlearn, re-learn, and re-learn.

"The more you read, the more you'll be able to know. The more you understand about the world, the further you'll visit." Dr. Seus

3). KNOW HOW TO HANDLE YOUR NEEDS AND WANTS

"Your ability to differentiate the needs and wants will assist you.

take the correct decisions. "-Bukola Sunday.

Your desires are to purchase goods or services, emotions, as well as other items we'd want but do not really need.

The things we need are the ones we need to be able survive like water, food, shelter, for example.

There's a vast distinction between what we desire in comparison to what we actually need. This is an example that is the best way to explain this.

We can't be without, like food. (i.e. We make sure that we obtain these items at the time we need them) and Wants are something that we are able to let go If we aren't able to take them right away, we could put off getting them at any point.

It is possible that you are wondering about which one is more significant between Wants and

You have needs, and this can help you.

* Wish -- feel the desire to have or accomplish (something) and wish for.

* Requirement -- need (something) as it's vital or extremely important, rather than merely desired.

There is nothing wrong with wanting to do it They are enjoyable, and in many cases, they can assist you to achieve important goals such as staying close to family members, enjoying yourself and staying fit. They aren't essential for your well-being or survival.

"Learning to make better choices and to differentiate between wants and needs will help you stay out of debt and reach financial freedom sooner"

For you to become successful, be aware of the things you require at any moment, and don't mess around with your requirements because of the things you desire. The pursuit of what you want in instead of what you require could result in you in a position of being mediocre.

If, for instance, you're required to register for a class at a cost of 4000 dollars (#4000) and you own an item of footwear that is at similar to the course you're supposed to enroll in What will you sign up to? the ability to discern exactly what you want and what you're looking for will assist you.

take the correct decision.

If you are able to make appropriate choices between your requirements and your wants, that you're ready to be important.

4). Maximize Opportunities

" Opportunity is A chance for advancement, progress or profit"--

Bukola Sunday

Opportunities can be viewed as a favorable situation or event, and could be considered to be a positive or favorable circumstance, or a mixture of circumstances.An chance only comes when they say it the word, if you don't take advantage of the opportunity, you could not be able to get it again, except in the event that God wills to favour your.

"A pessimist sees the difficulty in every opportunity; an optimist sees the opportunity in every difficulty." -Winston S. Churchill

Being valuable means embracing every opportunity to gain knowledge or gain new insights and meet new people. You can also be a part of making a difference in people's lives.

"If an potential opens up, do not pull back the shade."-Tom Peters

You want to begin setting up your own business or start a idea and require the equivalent of half a million dollars Start and you are approached by someone who wants to give you the identical amount, but you decline the offer because of your religious beliefs or beliefs are not in favor of borrowing money I'll tell you that you will begin your business in the future because you've missed an important possibility, but only if you already have the source you're looking for that exact amount from.

A single opportunity could transform your life, so to succeed, be prepared to take advantage of opportunities that arrive but you must be aware of the kind of opportunity you accept.

Certain people watch films all day long and some Zee the world while other are able to chat for seven hours. Are you wondering what possibilities can be found and I'm missing? If you are working on the above.

"A wise man will make more opportunities than he finds." -Francis Bacon

Let me say it straight If you wish to be considered valuable it is essential to take advantage of opportunities. You can achieve this through hard work.

"If opportunity doesn't knock, build a door." Milton Berle

Do you realize that you could make yourself more successful? how?

* If you're supposed to go through a book, do it!

If you're required to take part in a course, go to it!

Do you notice that if you're a knowledgeable person, people do not take you for granted? This means that you've established a place to yourself, as people are eager to hear your words.

"Opportunities tend to be hidden as work therefore, most people aren't aware of them."-Ann Landers

My best friend always says the moment you combine opportunity with preparation, it is a win-win situation and everyone who is successful and that are successful today were prepared to be successful, therefore prepare.

My Advice for you

"If somebody gives you an incredible opportunity however you're not certain you're able to take it on take it - and

Then, learn to master it later."-Richard Branson

5). See Failure As Success.

"If you make a mistake because of fear it will be made"-Bukola Sunday.

Today, it appears that failure is more likely to be more prominent than a successful one. That's at least the way we see it be. We often worry about it, do our best to keep it from happening We ponder our own thoughts each time we come up with new thoughts.

The reality is that no achievement was attained without a failure. There could be a single epic loss. or a sequence of mishaps including Edison's 10,000 tries to design the light bulb, or Dyson's 5,126 efforts to create the bagless vacuum cleaner. It doesn't matter if we enjoy the idea or not, failure is a crucial step in the direction of achieving our hopes.

"It's failure that gives you the proper perspective on success." Ellen DeGeneres. Ellen DeGeneres.

There is no way to be successful in life if fearful of failure, but would you tell me what is your definition of failing?

For me, failure is an chance to make the job done, failing is an opportunity for a second chance, Failure is a learning experience.

avenue to do more, etc. With this attitude, you're in the position to become highly valuable as you'll not hesitate to take advantage of opportunities or venture into areas that can be difficult to acquire.

"Success is most often achieved by those who don't know that failure is inevitable." Coco Chanel. Coco Chanel.

Do you ever wonder why? you ask yourself, Was it because #MarkZuckerberg and all the others absolutely certain that they'll succeed once they begin?

If you did not know the previous information, you should now know that failure itself is successful, and if you fail, you've achieved the ability to make things work when you decide to attempt the same thing over and over again. It is well-known that the man who invented the bulb that is now known as the electric Thomas Edison failed nine thousand nine hundred and ninety-nine times (9,999) before he achieved what he desired.

The first time he tried his hand at it but did not succeed, he discovered that the initial method would not allow the electricity to come into existence, so he kept going to work on it. Don't overlook the fact that he was insecure about failing the second time. Not until he mastered it Don't be scared of failing if you wish to succeed.

"If you're not prepared to be wrong, you'll never come up with anything original." -- Ken Robinson

6). Solve Problems

"A problem is a chance for you to do your best." Duke Ellington

"Knowing what you are good at and putting it into practice, help you solve problems around it" Bukola Sunday

The process of solving a question for which you have a solution is akin to climbing the mountain with a guide or following the path others have put in place. The truth in mathematics lies at a location that nobody is aware of, far from the paths that are well-worn. It's not always on the summit of the hill. There could be an opening in the most smooth mountain or deep within the valley.

If you aren't interested in working on problems, it's a sign that you're not prepared to be a successful businessperson You aren't ready to get noticed, make an impact on the world, and aren't ready to prove yourself important.

Today, we live in a society where if you don't have the ability to resolve any issue it's because your skills are in vain, and solving issues does not necessarily refer to family problems and so, get it.

If you are selling food, it solves the problem of food insecurity, while if you sell clothing, you are dealing with the issue of not having clothes. If you're a teacher and you solve an issue with illiteracy. While it's unlikely that all pupils you instruct are able to acquire the information they need to be able to master The most crucial aspect is that you're fixing a problem.

If you think that watching a movie can make you more valuable Think again. There is a plenty of time to do everything, but did you realize that the people you're viewing are creating names for themselves, and you're taking note of them. ?

Check out Dangote(Dangote, a Nigerian Entrepreneur) Is he not working on solving issues? He is indeed solving many problems. how? by selling his items that are demanded in various ways of life. It is impossible to miss one of his items in Nigeria.

If you don't like Dangote's cement but you don't have to be able to miss his salt or macro or salt, for instance. You can tell that he solves problems, and after he's solved the problems, you'll be paying the price, correct?.

Keep in mind that there are so many challenges in the world right now and you must begin to solve them If you're not sure something you can use to tackle those issues, find out the best way to tackle the problems. Since once you get started solving the difficulties, the cash will not chase you.

You are trying to make cash.

A problem-solver's mindset gives you a competitive edge at any location you go to because the people will be delighted to have you in the area and are confident they will not worry, therefore for you to stand out, resolve issues.

7) Think And Re-think

"Before you become millionaire, you need to learn how to think like one. Learn you can motivate yourself to overcome anxiety with courage." Thomas J. Stanley

"The the money lies in your creative genius, there's a country within your

imagination""Imagination" -Chris Ain

To think is to possess an active mind. It is certain extents of thinking or recalling events, making intelligent decisions, and evaluating the situation or addressing a specific scenario, or to possess an idea or shape in your mind an idea or thought.

"In critical thinking lies great innovations" --Bukola Sunday

The key to this isn't worry about circumstances but rather laying the foundations of new ideas or the foundations which can transform the world or even oneself.

Thinking here happens conscious and not in a vacuum.

"I have concluded that wealth is a state of mind and that anyone can acquire a wealthy state of mind by thinking rich thoughts." Edward

What was the last time you had a chance to consider your personal life, education and family life, even your own business? If you've never done this then please make time for some time to think and fix things, because most times we possess in-built talents. However, because we don't sit down and review our life, those talents diminish little by little. Remember that within your thinking is the source of great innovation and new ideas. So start to think.

There are a lot of individuals making waves in the world of today. Do you believe it's in the same way? No.

My guide Emmanuel Akpe will Always say that he is usually with the most powerful advisor on earth, which is holy.

Are you sure he received the message? This was simply due to being aware of the divine power.

It is my understanding that thinking is a process that requires some time to grow. Thinking and language have to integrate. Be aware that once this happens, something unique appears, so it is essential to develop a habit of thinking critically in order to change the world around you and be valuable.

"Money is everywhere, if it's not coming to you, engage in critical thinking"Bukola Sunday Bukola Sunday

8) Set Goals

"Never quit. It is the easiest cop-out in the world. Set a goal and don't quit until you attain it. When you do attain it, set another goal, and don't quit until you reach it. Never quit." -Bear Bryant

Goal setting goes not just about writing goals down, The goal is set and must have to be met.Set "SMART" goals Your objectives must be

* S-Specific

* M- Measurable

* A- Achievable

* R- Realistic

* T- Time-Bound

It is essential to have an exact outline of the goals you would like to accomplish, it helps you to focus and rapidity.

"The trouble with not having a goal is that you can spend your life running up and down the field and never score." -Bill Copeland

The process of setting goals and then striving to exceed these goals will set you up for being a person with a mission.

Assume that you've got the goal of earning 1 million in the course of six (6) months

What are the best ways to accomplish this?

1MILLION divided into 6 months, which is 166,666 for a month If you want to earn

1 million before this year is over then you'll need earn $166,666 each month to meet your goal. It's an estimate, but the exact number is unclear at this point. We've determined the amount we'll need to earn in a single month to reach the goal.

target.

The next step is to figure out what is required to SELL in order in order to earn that cash. This is how we find the idea

The monthly target is 166,666

The next step is figure out HOW much of that Item that we will need to market in order to figure out the quantity.

For example, if you are planning to sell 50 items. Divide the monthly goal by 50.

167,000 / 50 = N3,340

Today, N3,340 is the cost of one piece of products you have to sell. It is also necessary to sell at minimum 50 of them each month. All you have to find out if that you could sell from N3,340 to 50 people each month.

In the event that you fail to get together with the 50 people, you'll have be able to pay for the following month. The product you're selling could be a product or service. It's not difficult to earn one million dollars in the coming year. This is the time to discover that item or service which will earn cash.

"Don't just set goals to be intentional rugged about it"Bukola Bukola Bukola

Sunday

9) TIME MANAGEMENT & CONVERSION

"Rich people use money to purchase additional time, whereas those who are poor spend their time trying for more money."-Bukola Sunday

"A person who is willing to spend a single minute hasn't realized the worth of existence."-Charles Darwin

If you are looking to become something of value in the market, then put an emphasis to the time. It is an indispensible resource and time is the sole source of currency that exists in the world. The principle that governs timing is that time needs to be transformed into items. This is not just about products, but rather valuable products.

There are three ways to utilize time

a. You could waste it.

b. You could use it to spend.

C. You could put it to work

The time wasted by fools is wasted, average people have time to do things, but smart people put their time into it.

How can you make time?

It is a time-consuming process of creating value for yourself by listening to books, reading and learning skills.

• You spend your time creating value for others by coaching, teaching, or mentoring.

The time you invest in producing products with value (or value chain. You are creating products that prove you're using your time effectively

"The only difference between a rich person and a poor person is how they use their time." Robert Kiyosaki

Benjamin Franklin said: Does this person love living? Don't waste precious time because that's what you need to do in that life is.

The value you can add to your life is through timing conversion. When you are aware of time conversion, you won't allow a minute to pass through without turning the time into value for you.

"Every each day has a banking account and time is our money. Nobody is wealthy or poor. We have access to every day of the week." Christopher Rice

11) Live A Life You Can Afford

Our society is in a state where many of us feel sad and angry over the images that our acquaintances post through social media. They then spend our resources to be just like them, and to achieve their standards.

Manage your spending, one of the simplest things to accomplish in life is spend. There are numerous publications and conferences on ways to save money and invest, however there's no advice on how you can make money.

A lifestyle that is pleasing to other people, but is putting financial pressure on you is not going to help you achieve your goals or be successful in your life.

In the end, after working on everything previously mentioned issues It is important to be a hard worker However, it's best to be SMART and foremost, don't forget God throughout the process. Consider Him to be your primary guide! He is the only one who has the entire set of keys.

Chapter 18: What Is Money?

Webster Definition of money. anything that is generally recognized as a means for exchange, or a measurement of value, or way to pay: for example, official coined or stamped new money that has been minted.

NOW I WILL SHARE WITH YOU THE DEFINITION AND WHAT SOME IMPORTANT PEOPLE TODAY SAY ABOUT MONEY.

ALIKO DANGOTE, one of the wealthiest men in Africa says "Money doesn't have color whether you are in Africa or anywhere in the world the color of money is the same."

MARK ZUCKERBERG, the founder of Facebook states "Simply put; we don't build services to make money, we make money to build services"

Based on our definitions and quotations from our definitions and quotes, we can conclude that money isn't just an exchange of currency. It is the value you utilize in buying something or purchasing something specific, but money transcends currency, but everything that you exchange for the form of something is called money.

Value is what you make So, you need to ask yourself, is my worth money? Can my value create wealth? It is possible, and it is discussed in the final section of the book. When you know the meaning of money, we can discuss where the money is hiding.

Chapter 19: Where Does Money Hide?

1). The money is hidden in ideas and seeds.

2). Money hides in work.

3.) 3. Money Hides in terms of value.

1). Money Hides In Ideas And Seeds.

The world is ruled by ideas, every aspect of our lives was born from an idea. I'm referring to every aspect. The Holy BIBLE talks about GOD being a thinker before He created man, so let us create man according to the image of God was an concept.

"All wealth has its roots in the mind. It's all in the ideas, not money." Robert Collier

Mark Zuckerberg had an idea to develop the social media platform on which students could interact with one others and also with their colleagues This is an idea.

Ah, I'm in need of an efficient transportation system that is able to travel very quickly and aren't a problem for transportation caused by air transport It's an idea.

"All achievements, all earned riches, have their beginning in an idea." Napoleon Hill

Instead of of going to the store face to face when buying their product should we not create a platform which allows customers to purchase products without having to meet sellers, and thus bringing online marketing.

Many examples you could imagine, each business began with an idea.Ideas come by the brain and the only way to generate excellent ideas is to use inventive thinking. Ideas are among the most secretive areas where the money is kept, as ideas are the foundation of every business.

Once you've identified an idea that you're working on create that concept which is what we can be called Seed. Here's a formula that I'd like to show your mind. MIND + CREATIVE THINK = IDEA. Once you understand the idea's implementation will transform into seeds. And the seeds that grow will result in money.

In all of the formulas this is probably among them. It's the ALMIGHTY method to determine where the money is hidden, since all you observe in our world that generates cash follows the same pattern.

The most costly mistake you take today is not pursuing to implement that idea you have in your mind. Don't sit around waiting until someone else thinks of the concept you've come up with and then implement it. You may regret your decision later. When you read this article, I am sure you have some idea that is running through your thoughts Don't let it go create a seeds and, when it matures and grows, money will flow from it.

2). Money Hides In Work

Money is work, it is work and it requires working. To earn this cash, you must do your best. This isn't a lazy man's work, all the things you listed is a must, so work for these goals and you will always remain far away.

You have the money. You're not far away from it Don't spend your time on unneeded things. Invest your time and energy into making money, and adhere to the rules that are laid out. Money will never leave your grasp.

3. Money Hides In Value

The term "value" is a synonym for value. The value refers to the amount that a certain item or person.

The way you market is determined by value If you think about the seven places that money hides. You can see that to earn the money you need, you have to become an entrepreneur, which implies you need to market some thing, be it your talents, gifts or product, an idea, or whatever else you can come up with.

Marketing, the term "value" is measured as the distinction between the prospective customer experience as well as the price of a service when compared with other. Simply put, the relation between perceived advantages and cost;

therefore, I'll create the formula below that

Value = benefits/cost

The worth of the items you offer, whether your services, products or ideas, gift cards, and more, will determine the value you can earn.

* Low value means small amount of money

* Value high = huge sum of money

Your place in worth determines the amount you receive, and to earn greater wealth, and to add more worth in your existence.

The places I have listed are only a few of the areas where money hides. Money is also able to hide in the solution of problems.

Chapter 20: What Can Buy Money?

"If you didn't have to use cash now, could you still live and survive?" If you are beginning your journey towards financial independence You must keep three things in your mind,

* What is the amount you like to have by your name?

Money is not the aim; it's not the goal. being financially secure

The goal is freedom.

* . Financial freedom is something you should consider.

My instructor Tobe Onwordi was the one to ask the following question during a class session: If you did not require cash at present and you could still exist and make it through the day?

One student told me that I don't think that way, sir. That indicates that there is a major issue. We have switched our focus away from the root to the result, but What do I mean? Based on the idea of the batter-trade method, we are able to tell that the actual money is not the money we think of now and it's definitely not. instead of focusing on what is actually cash, we've focused on the effect on the money.

Richard Bronson was asked what company he would create if he were only left with 5 dollars?

In addition the man who owns Virgin Atlantic, can you figure out what his answer was?

If he were a typical Nigerian I'm certain that he'd say perhaps start selling the purest water, rice or something else.

Richard Bronson said something that stunned me.

The man said he'd personally sign the item and then sell it at $20. He'd repeat the process to

Take the money and earn $100.

What will we think of when we ask him about the way he was using to purchase cash? Richard Bronson said if he was given a note of $5 to begin a new business, the note would be signed by him and then sell it at 20 dollars. He would then do similar procedure with the other $20.

I was just as awestruck as you were when I learned that. It has made me think about money as a other product on the market is a commodity that can be purchased! !

When we look at the story of Richard Bronson, which do we think he'll be using for selling the 20 and 100 dollars?

Is it logical buying money at a higher price? No, I'm not sure. If you're acquainted with Richard Bronson, you would be aware that he's an entrepreneur and, over time, he's grown in popularity in the market because of (WHO He is).

It wasn't his first choice to do it this way. If the time came that it was perhaps when he was in his teens and such, he'd be unsuccessful in convincing someone to trade more dollars in exchange in exchange for "less" dollars.

Was there anything that had changed about Richard Bronson so that he could have enough confidence in doing this? Absolutely WHO He had become over the top and HE SERVED the public.

"When your values are clear to you, making decisions becomes easier." Roy E. Disney .

To become a successful buyer of money you need to know how to increase an amount of net wealth. Net worth is the sum of your contribution to the world around you and also your globe.

The value of your net worth is measured by the number of people who require you, and the issues you solve. It defines your worth as well as its resemblance to the world.

Everyone was born with worth. However, no one has an estimated net worth. The self-worth of you is different than the value of your net. Self-worth is the value you have as a human being, however the net worth you have built is what makes it. Self-worth will eventually be insignificant without having a net worth.

People only care about the people who have constructed their net worth. Remember, we're not just discussing money or assets today, but rather the entirety of your worthiness.

What are the best ways to build an amount of wealth?

a. Explore your purpose in this life:

Pay a lot of your attention to you. Be attentive to the conversations in your soul, and you'll find that. Your own discovery makes you significant to your community. The real you is not the name you've been named, but the name you accept. Example mentioning Nelson Mandela defines it, Martin Luther, etc.

b. Be a professional: occupy the time you have to your work.

C. Inspire your own skills: learn a skills

D. Develop a product with worth

E. Learn more.

I'll tell you a little story about myself, following getting my ND (National Degree) from Federal Polytechnic Auchi (Edo state) Nigeria. I was in Lagos and stayed there for 3 years. in Lagos. I then decided to return to Niger state. I went in a limb for a few months without work while walking along an alley one day and discovered a job posting advertisement, and I chose to apply for the position when I got to the firm (Nakowa Savings and Investment Company Ltd). We were among the top three (30) individuals who attended for an interview. you know what? I was the only person to be offered the job and I am sure you'll be asking yourself how this was possible? Now I'll tell you.

In the course of my National Diploma, final year specifically, I was working in a co-operative that did exactly what this business is planning to do prior to the interview, I was required go back to all the things I'd learnt from the place I had worked prior to.

In the course of the interview, the questions and responses were being exchanged like usual. However, they realize that by the manner in which I answered questions, it appeared like I knew the goal they wanted to accomplish and was speaking like I owned the cooperative.

It is evident that I have shared my Who I Am through the worth I've received from my work environment and how I've grown as a person.

It is possible to buy things through your personality So, work hard to make sure your net worth will surpass cash.

Understanding what you can purchase with money is essential, however the main thing to consider is managing your money once you receive it.

The 20's can be a time of the making of big decisions in your life. Which career direction will you take? Are you going to a higher education institution? The most important and crucial option that is often overlooked can be Money Management. How do you manage your finances? What decisions do you take regarding your financial situation? Will the outcome affect you in the present or negative for many years in the future?

In particular, a poor credit score may make it difficult to achieve goals like buying a house or investing in a good way, or obtaining business loans. The burden of debt and financial issues could cause stress to decrease and stop you from taking risks. So, it is important to establish the right budget and be aware of the amount you spend. Create financial goals that you can meet by doing this, it will assist you with balancing your financial situation.

Chapter 21: How Value Brings Money?

The rules:

First GIVE OUT VALUE.

It is the tangible thing that you can buy. is the money you take out placing intangible value.

"The more often you give to others in return, the greater amount of money is going to

You will be rewarded. "-Emmanuel Akpe

Value = benefits/cost

The worth of the product you offer, be it product, service, idea or gifts you can determine the amount of the money you can earn. Low value = low money. High value = large cash

Therefore, you must create value for the product you offer. Everyone wants to earn money, but do you realize that it is not every person who can make the cash? It's because, while it's every person who is looking to fix the issue, and some feel content with the situation they're at. Certain people are dependent on the wealth of their families.

Open your eyes. Do you think that if your life doesn't hold value, it is impossible to be a successful manager of wealth, even when you are able to get it no cost? If you're valuable, you'll be able manage wealth and will also be productive.

How can value be a source of income?

Value can be a source of money in many ways. For instance, when I design an advertisement for you and it's stunning, you'll make me a payment, which is because I've solved a issue that you had.

In the event that you eat at the restaurant, you have to purchase the food because you have no hunger problem. This line represents your contribution to earn cash to you. You must provide a service.

An act that provides aid to anyone.

If you can solve a challenge, you will receive some reward or it comes from the person whom you provided those services to, or God In either way you could or might be rewarded to solve the issue. If you wish to increase your worth in return for money perform services, you must. More services you offer and the higher your earnings receive.

"If you are looking for your contribution in order to generate income for you then you should avoid

procrastination". - Bukola Sunday

Procrastination refers to the practice of delaying, postponing or postponing, especially regularly or deliberately. Procrastination slows the process and impacts the likelihood of becoming efficient.

What's the difference between silver, gold and bronze? In the end, they're all gemstones, but with different characteristics. However, gold is more valuable than silver and bronze is more valuable than silver. When something is valued highly, it will become scarce. When things are scarce, they become extremely valuable. This is the answer to what makes gold of more value? It is so valuable that everybody wants it making it rare and only available to certain individuals, so and that means people must start digging deep, and don't be able to ignore the negative consequences.

One of my friends went to a gold mining site and was informed the place was previously utilized for the cultivation of cocoa due to the fertility of the soil. They had to remove all cocoa when they found out that the area was contaminated with gold.

The human being can be much more appreciated than gold, and also the most costly material in the universe (antimatter) in the event that he is extremely respected. It is possible to decide to put the value of yourself, but it won't be as high as what value is placed on you by other people. They'll do everything to win you over, they could dig up the earth from the earth in order in order to get you. They are willing to pay you whatever sum you want to bring you over to their side. No doubt it is the strength of the word "VALUE.

The value of your life can turn you into an item of treasure that are so rare that everybody will seek the one of you. People from around the globe are searching for you.

A fascinating aspect of worth is the fact that a person who owns a possession may not realize the value of his possessions. They might choose to dispose of it or donate the item to someone else, and when it's the property by the right person, the item is valued greatly. It happens to a few people working or with relationships.

To be appreciated than silver and antimatter as well as an extremely valuable precious treasure. It is essential to have appealing and attractive characteristics. Everyone has these types of qualities that could be very valuable, however often they are not to be found.

You just need to conduct a thorough soul search and you'll discover your treasures.

www.ingramcontent.com/pod-product-compliance
Lightning Source LLC
Chambersburg PA
CBHW070734020526
44118CB00035B/1344